Lay Speaking Ministries

Lay Speaking Ministries

Basic Course
Participant's Book

Sandy Zeigler Jackson with Brian Jackson

DISCIPLESHIP RESOURCES

PO BOX 340003 • NASHVILLE, TN 37203-0003
www.discipleshipresources.org

Cover design by Paul Gant

Interior design by PerfectType, Nashville, TN

ISBN 978-0-88177-552-5

Library of Congress Catalog in Publication 2008909809

Paragraph numbers included in this text refer to the 2004 edition of The Book of Discipline of The United Methodist Church.

Third Printing: 2009

Contents

Introduction

God calls you to a life of servanthood as a disciple of Jesus Christ. You are reading this study because you have felt a gentle touch or a strong push to pursue your call to serve the church in a greater capacity. Lay Speaking Ministries is the first step for many laity to begin their faith journey or to strive for a closer relationship with the Lord. Lay Speaking Ministries will give you many opportunities to serve your local and the greater church. The ministries of Lay Speaking are caring, leading, and communicating.

We can all find a calling in one or more of these areas of ministry. This class will familiarize you with these areas of ministry and give you a chance to explore each one. Upon completion of this course, we hope that you will see the area God is calling you to pursue. The United Methodist Church depends upon its laity to carry out its missions and purpose. Your local church and pastor depend on you as laity to pursue and accomplish their purpose of making disciples. Many journeys of deepening faith and service in ministry have begun with this class. Enjoy and be open to God's call upon your life.

Session One

Ministry of the Baptized

But you are a chosen race, a royal priesthood, a holy nation, God's own people, in order that you may proclaim the mighty acts of him who called you out of darkness into his marvelous light. Once you were not a people, but now you are God's people; once you had not received mercy, but now you have received mercy (1 Peter 2:9-10).

Learning Outcome Goals:

At the end of this session the participant will be able to:

1. Describe the reality of the priesthood of all believers and God's call on our lives;
2. Discuss spiritual gifts; meaning and purpose;
3. Describe the need for a response to God's call;
4. Discuss the early Methodist movement and the role of laity.

United Methodist Background

United Methodists share basic affirmations of the Christian faith with other Christian communities. They are:

- We hold in common with all Christians a faith in the mystery of salvation in and through Jesus Christ;
- We share the Christian belief that God's redemptive love is realized in human life by the activity of the Holy Spirit, both in personal experience and in the community of believers;
- We understand ourselves to be part of Christ's universal church when by adoration, proclamation, and service we become conformed to Christ;
- With other Christians we recognize that the reign of God is both a present and future reality;
- We share with many other Christian communions a recognition of the authority of scripture in matters of faith, the confession that our justification as sinners is by grace through faith, and the sober realization that the church is in need of continual reformation and renewal.

Wesleyan Emphases

There are distinct Wesleyan emphases that shape who we are as United Methodists. John Wesley believed that it was not enough to believe or have faith but that faith and love should be put into practice in our lives.

One of the main emphases of Methodism is grace. "By grace we mean that undeserved, unmerited, and loving action of God" (*The Book of Discipline of the United Methodist Church, 2004* ¶101). Wesley further described grace as:

Prevenient—the grace that causes our first thoughts of God and draws us to God;

Justifying—the grace from God that is willing to accept us and forgive us, "just as if" we had never sinned;

Sanctifying—the grace that continues to nurture us and to increase our knowledge so that we can more fully love God and our neighbor. We are committed to "go on to perfection" by having a heart "habitually filled with the love of God and neighbor" and by "having the mind of Christ and walking as he walked."

Another Wesleyan emphasis is faith and good works. We exhibit our faith as we respond to the gift of salvation by our works of piety and mercy. Our personal salvation is evidenced when we join our hearts and hands in mission and service.

The emphasis on mission and service happens when we hold in balance our "scriptural holiness" or personal piety, act of devotion and worship, and our "social holiness" or acts of compassion and justice.

The mission of the church is one of nurture and outreach. Our faith is nurtured by the church through Christian fellowship and participation in a worshiping community. The church equips us for mission and service in our communities and in the world.

We are blessed as individuals and a denomination when we emphasize these Wesleyan principles in living out our faith.

A Connectional Church

The United Methodist Church is a connectional church through our polity, our ties to other United Methodist churches, and our basic Christian beliefs and values. This connectionalism is based on a mutual responsiveness to each other and the world and on

Notes

Notes

accountability to God and each other at all levels of the church.

Ministry happens throughout the church and the world through our apportionments, our appointment system for clergy, and our mutual efforts in missions. More importantly, we are connected by the Spirit of Christ and as brothers and sisters by prayerful concern for each other as we watch over one another with love.

The Priesthood of Believers

> But you are a chosen race, a royal priesthood, a holy nation . . . (1 Peter 2:9).

What does it mean to be a member of a priesthood? In Old Testament times, a priest acted as a mediator between the people and God because sinful people did not approach God directly. The priests performed the ministry as instructed by God, and they offered sacrifices on behalf of the people. But with Christ and his victory over sin and death, we can now come into God's presence without the intermediary priest. We are now charged with the obligation to declare God's wondrous act of salvation to others. Because of our relationship with Christ, we can represent him to others just as the ancient priest represented God to the people. We are indeed a chosen people, chosen as God's very own.

Our priesthood or ministry does not depend on what we do but on who we are in Christ. We are saints from every tribe and language and people and nation, ransomed by Christ, and he has made us to be a kingdom and priests serving our God (Revelation 5: 9-10).

Through Christ we have full access to God because he is our high priest, who offered himself in sacrifice on our behalf. So, all believers are priests in the kingdom of God, laity and clergy. Any distinction between lay and clergy comes from our ministry roles within the church.

The priesthood of believers does not deny order, authority,

10

Notes

or discipline within our churches. The offices for preaching, teaching, administering the sacraments, and equipping the saints are still viable in our denomination. But it does deny the notion of spiritual elitism. We are all one in Christ and are members of the priesthood of believers. And we are all called to proclaim God's wonder and works in bringing us out of the darkness of sin into God's marvelous light.

Exploring God's Call

Have you heard God's call on your life? You probably have, in one way or another, or you wouldn't be taking this course for leadership in the church.

The Bible records how God worked through many people and events:

God called Moses from a burning bush.

God called Samuel through a voice in the night.

God called Esther through her cousin Mordecai.

Isaiah saw a vision and heard God ask whom he should send.

God sent an angel to Mary to reveal the plan for her to bear God's son. And God spoke to Joseph in a dream as he worried about Mary's situation concerning Mary.

God called Saul through a blinding light on the road to Damascus, and he was blind until Ananias laid hands on him.

Here are some other calls recorded in the Bible:

God called Abraham in the midst of his success and Jacob in the midst of his failure.

Notes

God called Sarah to bear a son when she thought it was impossible. In fact, she laughed at the notion. Then came Isaac.

God called Gideon repeatedly and provided the proof he needed.

God called Amos, a herdsman.

God called Jeremiah before he was born.

God called Elijah through a still small voice.

God called Peter, James, and John with a quiet "follow me."

God called Martha out of the busyness of the kitchen.

God called Matthew from his tax collection table and Zaccheus from the sycamore tree.

God called a gentile foreigner on the road to Gaza, a woman at a well in Samaria, a Canaanite woman who dared to argue with Jesus, and a thief hanging next to Jesus on the cross.

God continues to call people although the biblical canon has been closed. Through songs of the children next door, God called the young man who became Augustine of Hippo. God called Martin Luther through a thunderstorm, and John Wesley's heart was strangely warmed as he heard someone reading aloud Luther's preface to Romans.

God has called many others throughout the centuries, and that includes you! How is God calling you? Maybe you didn't actually hear the voice of God, but perhaps you heard another lay speaker talk about ministry, or your pastor made a suggestion.

Hearing God's Call

How do we distinguish the voice of God calling us to service? Think about all the calls you get—telemarketers, friends, family, business associates, etc. Think about all the names people call you—Mom, Dad, brother, sister. We're called so often that it may be difficult to hear God's call. Like Samuel (1 Samuel 3), it may sound like the voice of our pastor or a spiritual friend. But could it be God?

Soren Kierkegaard wrote in his journal, "what I really lack is to be clear in my mind what I am to do, not what I am to know . . . .The thing is to understand what God really wishes me to do . . . ." (Sue Annis Hammond, *The Thin Book of Appreciative Inquiry* [Bend, OR: Thin Book Publishing Co., 1998], 20-21).

> Beloved, do not believe every spirit, but test the spirits to see whether they are from God . . . (1 John 4:1).

Take the time to listen for God's voice. Jesus often left the disciples and crowds and went to quiet places to spend time with God, to hear God's voice. There are processes that can help us determine whether the "voice" we have heard or the experience we have had or the opportunity that presents itself is a call from God. The process is called discernment, which means "to separate," "to sort out," "to sift through" our interior and exterior experiences to find the source of the call and an appropriate response.

Here are some attitudes of heart that should be present during the time of discernment:

1. Trust. "Commit your way to the LORD; trust in him, and he will act" (Ps. 37:5). We trust that God is present with us, loves us, and has work for us to do.
2. Listening. "Be still and know that I am God" (Ps. 46:10). We need to spend time in quiet with open hearts and minds to hear the voice of God.

Notes

3. Prayer. "Seek the L ORD and his strength; seek his presence continually" (Ps. 105:4). Don't do all the talking in prayer. Ask God for wisdom and guidance. Listen.

4. Seek Information. "If you continue in my word . . . you will know the truth" (John 8:31-32). Study the experiences of others and the ways God has communicated in their lives.

5. Humility. "He leads the humble in what is right, and teaches the humble his way" (Ps. 25:9). Humility comes from drawing near to God where we can sense our own incompleteness.

6. Purity of Purpose. "Blessed are the pure in heart, for they will see God" (Mt. 5:8). Be sure that you are sincere and not influenced by perceived notions of importance or power in your call or your own self-interests.

7. Discipline and Perseverance. ". . . those who seek me diligently find me" (Prov. 8:17). Be disciplined in your attempts to hear God's voice in the silence. Be diligent in setting side the time for this experience.

8. Patience and Urgency. "Be still before the L ORD, and wait patiently" (Ps. 37:7). Waiting patiently does not mean doing nothing. Continue to study and pray, but maintain a sense of urgency in understanding the direction of your path.

9. Perspective. "They served their idols which became a snare to them" (Ps. 106:36). Watch for obstacles such as security, human timeframes, self-doubt, and self-righteousness.

(Adapted from Farnham, Gill, McLean, Ward, *Listening Hearts: Discerning Call in Community* [Harrisburg, PA: Morehouse Publishing, 1991], 29-37.)

Responding to God's Call

Listening and responding to God's call is vital to our relationship with God. Have you ever called a child who did not respond? Remember how frustrated you felt? When God calls, we must be ready to respond and act upon what we are told.

God called Jonah to go to Nineveh. Jonah's response was to flee in the opposite direction. However, God gained Jonah's attention, and he finally did what God wanted. How much easier it would have been if Jonah had responded like Isaiah and said, "Here I am, send me." When God calls us to service, there is a purpose.

Moses turned aside to investigate the phenomenon of the burning bush, and because he turned aside, he heard God's call. Moses answered, "Here I am." God used him to lead the Israelites out of Egypt. Samuel did as Eli advised him and responded to God's call by saying, "Speak, for your servant is listening." God then used Samuel as a prophet to the nation Israel.

Esther was in a unique position to affect the judgments of the king. Mordecai suggested to Esther that she might have come to her royal position "for such a time as this." Because she listened, she was able to keep the Jews from being persecuted by Haman.

The stories of call and response continue throughout the Bible and beyond. In most cases the responses were immediate and without excuses. May your response be "Here I am, Lord; send me."

The purpose of the church is to make disciples, and that requires that people respond to the will of God in their lives. Our primary task is to reach out to people in our communities and world and to receive them into the church. In the church, we relate those people to God, nurturing them and strengthening their Christian faith. But it doesn't stop there! Those very same people—*we*, the people—are to live transformed lives and to reach out and receive others. To accomplish God's work in the world and in the church, we must hear and respond to the call.

Notes

Spiritual Gifts

EQUIPPED WITH GIFTS

God does not expect you to go out into the world unprepared or unequipped. The Holy Spirit gives gifts in order to equip you for service. These spiritual gifts come from the Holy Spirit. There is a difference between the gift of the Holy Spirit and the gifts of the Holy Spirit. All Christians receive the gift of the Holy Spirit at the time of their conversion to Jesus Christ. Peter, the apostle, said, "Repent, and be baptized every one of you in the name of Jesus Christ so that your sins may be forgiven; and you will receive the gift of the Holy Spirit" (Acts 2:38). In John 3:6 we learn that believing Christians are "born of the Spirit." Ephesians 1:13 tells us we are "marked with the seal" of the Holy Spirit. (See also Eph. 4:5, Acts 11:15-16, 1 Cor. 6:19.) (Sue Annis Hammond, *The Thin Book of Appreciative Inquiry* [Bend, OR: Thin Book Publishing Co., 1998]).

The Holy Spirit is a gift that imparts other gifts to each Christian. These spiritual gifts wide variety and you can find descriptions in Romans 12, 1 Corinthians 12, and Ephesians 4. Many of the gifts are listed in these scripture passages, but only God knows the limitless variety of gifts.

The Holy Spirit gives spiritual gifts ". . . to equip the saints for the work of ministry, for building up the body of Christ, until all of us come to the unity of the faith and of the knowledge of the Son of God, to maturity, to the measure of the full stature of Christ" (Ephesians 4:10-13).

Spiritual gifts are specifically endowed by the Holy Spirit to equip us for ministry. Our gifts give us the skills and power we need for our specific ministries. When we discover our gifts, we can get a better sense of God's will for our lives and how we can best serve. We are more effective and efficient in our ministry when we use our spiritual gifts. Using our gifts demonstrates the presence of Christ in our lives.

SPIRITUAL GIFTS ARE:

- Unmerited blessings from God
- Job descriptions for ministries
- Means for discovering God's will
- Guarantees of effective service
- Means to efficient service
- Securities for health and growth
- Revealed presence of the living Christ
- Guarantor of lasting results

SPIRITUAL GIFTS ARE NOT:

- Acquired skills or natural talents
- Roles or offices
- For self-gain or division
- Fruits of the Spirit
- The same for everyone

Notes

People often confuse spiritual gifts with natural skills or talents. Our human skills or talents do not depend on the Holy Spirit's power but on our own abilities. People who are not Christians may have these same or similar skills or talents. To receive a certain gift, no matter how much we practice, we can never be good enough. God gives spiritual gifts, and our human desires do not bind God.

Often we think that someone has a specific gift for ministry because of his or her office or position within the church. A church-instituted role or office does not guarantee that the holder of that office or role has a specific spiritual gift. God does not intend gifts only for certain roles and offices but for *all* Christians.

Spiritual gifts benefit the whole church. We are not to become prideful about our spiritual gifts. Moreover, spiritual

Notes

gifts do not divide the church—they should bring the church together into one body empowered for ministry.

There is a difference between spiritual gifts and fruit of the Spirit (love, joy, peace, patience, kindness, goodness, faithfulness, gentleness, and self-control—see Gal. 4). The fruits of the Spirit relates to who we are and affect our relationships and the spiritual quality of our lives. Spiritual gifts, however, relate to what we do, our calling and function in ministry.

THE BODY OF CHRIST

Not everyone has the same gifts. If we did, how would God accomplish all of the ministry to the world? The apostle Paul relates our different spiritual gifts to the parts of the human body. Without all the parts, the body does not function well. So it is with spiritual gifts: without the use of all of the spiritual gifts, used, the church fails to function well.

EQUIPPED FOR GOOD DEEDS

> For we are what he has made us, created in Christ Jesus for good works, which God prepared beforehand to be our way of life (Ephesians 2:10).

The gifts of the Holy Spirit are our resources to prepare us for our various ministries and for doing good deeds. When we use these gifts as God intends, they affect our worship, Bible study, prayer, witnessing, and power.

The church at authentic worship requires the presence and operation of all the gifts, not just those operated by the minister and musicians. It is a coming together of the body parts to celebrate unity of power, position, and purpose. When we receive and use the spiritual gifts for their intended purposes, the Bible becomes a living study guide for holy and holistic living. We are attracted to a deeper prayer life as we recognize and use the spiritual gifts in our midst.

As persons realize that God has designed and given them special abilities for the general health and ministry within the Body of Christ, they become more joyfully motivated to share freely with others. Witnessing may be done by using our gifts in service to others. Because the power comes from God, and our new life in Christ gives us the power to overcome certain aspects of the evil forces in the world.

USING SPIRITUAL GIFTS

Like good stewards of the manifold grace of God, serve one another with whatever gift each of you has received. Whoever speaks must do so as one speaking the very words of God; whoever serves must do so with the strength that God supplies, so that God may

Some of the Spiritual Gifts

- Prophecy
- Pastoring
- Teaching
- Wisdom
- Knowledge
- Exhortation
- Discernment
- Giving
- Helping
- Mercy
- Mission
- Service
- Spirit-Music
- Craftsmanship
- Exorcism
- Miracles
- Evangelism
- Hospitality
- Faith
- Leadership
- Administration
- Suffering
- Healing
- Prayer Language
- Interpretation
- Apostleship
- Singleness
- Intercessory Prayer
- Martyrdom
- Battling
- Humor
- Voluntary Poverty

Notes

Notes

be glorified in all things through Jesus Christ (1 Peter 4:10-11).

God gives us these extraordinary abilities not to hide under a bushel or to stow away in a closet but to use them in service to God and neighbor. Spiritual gifts are in effect as long as the Spirit fills us. God calls us to be salt and light. If we lose our "saltiness," our gifts will be ineffective.

John Wesley encouraged Methodists to participate in the "Ordinances of God," also called "Means of Grace." They are the actions of Christians that keep them in relationship with Christ and exhibit their faith in their lives. By practicing these ordinances, we can maintain a balanced, holistic, Spirit-filled lives.

The Ministry of All Christians

> Christian ministry is the expression of the mind and mission of Christ by a community of Christians that demonstrates a common life of gratitude and devotion, witness and service, celebration and discipleship. All Christians are called through their baptism to this ministry of servanthood in the world to the glory of God and for human fulfillment. The forms of this ministry are diverse in locale, in interest, and in denominational accent . . . (*The Book of Discipline*, ¶125).

Christian ministry is sharing and living the love of Jesus Christ. At our baptism, we (or our parents on our behalf) covenanted with God that we would "serve as Christ's representatives in the world" (See Baptismal Covenant I, *The United Methodist Book of Worship*).

This is the heart of Christian ministry—to share Christ's love in the world. Christian ministry happens in many forms and locations, but the purpose and message remain the same. John Wesley described the character of a Methodist in this way:

Consequently, whatever a Methodist does, it is all to the glory of God. In all his efforts of every kind, he not only aims at this, (which is implied in having a single eye), but actually attains it. His work and recreation, as well as his prayers, all serve this great end. Whether he sits in his house or walks by the way, whether he lie down or rise up, he is promoting, in all he speaks or does, the one business of his life. Whether he put on his clothes, or work, or eat and drink, or entertain himself from hard labor, it all tends to advance the glory of God, by peace and good-will among men. His one invariable rule is this, "Whatever you do, in word or deed, do it all in the name of the Lord Jesus, giving thanks to God the Father by him" (Colossians 3:17). (John Wesley, *Character of a Methodist*.)

The ministry of the laity is a frontline ministry because laypersons have direct access to the community and access to settings that clergy do not normally have.

Somewhere in church history and tradition the church began to endow certain rights, privileges, and responsibilities of ministry to clergy. Clergy became the enlightened leadership, and laity became an audience, consumers of religion. But that's not the way it was intended to be.

It is time that laity took their role in ministry seriously and that all laity within the church accept, celebrate, and use the gifts of ministry.

Faithful Ministry

The people of God, who are the church made visible in the world, must convince the world of the reality of the gospel or leave it unconvinced. There can be no evasion or delegation of this responsibility; the church is either faithful as a witnessing and serving community, or it loses its vitality and its impact on an unbelieving world (*The Book of Discipline* ¶128).

Notes

Notes

God calls every Christian to be faithful in ministry. We are the church made visible in the world, and it is our responsibility to let the world know who Jesus Christ is. We cannot delegate this responsibility, nor can we evade it. Ministry is both a gift and a task that requires unstinting service.

It is important that the clergy and the laity live out their ministry as they have been gifted and called whether in the factory or in the hospital, at work or at home, in the church or in the community.

All God's People in
All Places,
And in
All Times,
Are Called to Love
And to Serve.

Ministry of the Laity

Your Response

Take some time to think about all that you have learned so far. Then write your response to the following questions:

1. In what ways have you heard God's call in your life?
2. How have you responded to that call?
3. What gifts do you sense that you have for the ministry of all Christians?

Wesleyan Tradition

The ministry of the laity was the backbone of early Methodism. John Wesley organized the people converted under his ministry to provide a way for them to grow in grace and to attain holiness. Wesley's organizational genius created three groups: societies, classes, and bands. Societies were large groups where God's Spirit could work to awaken and convict people, where they were connected with the prevenient grace of God, and where they could meet weekly for prayer, exhortation, and mutual care. To be a member of a society, one did not have to be a Christian. Societies included multiple classes. The Class Meeting was a smaller gathering, generally no more than twelve members. There was more of a family atmosphere in these settings. These class meetings provided the basis for stewardship and mission. Participants were required to pay a penny a week and a shilling per quarter. The money was used for the poor. The rules of the societies and class meetings were strict, but Wesley believed that there could be no spiritual maturity without discipline.

The bands were smaller groups that consisted of five to eight members of a class meeting. Wesley believed that spiritual formation occurred when people of the same gender met to discuss matters of the spiritual life and how to live it.

This approach simply makes sense. We read and study the Bible, but what do we *do* with it? It's what we *do* that makes what we study real and alive! Our faith results in human activity. Personal salvation always involves Christian mission and service to the world. We share our faith with others by serving and witnessing to our friends, family, neighbors, and the world.

Early Methodism relied heavily on the ministry of the laity. The circuit riders who preached the gospel from one place to another were not always able to tend to the congregation's needs. Therefore, the laity responded by caring for the community.

Notes

Notes

EXHORTERS AND CLASS LEADERS

Exhorters and class leaders led the Class or Band Meetings. They led prayer, addressed people on the subject of religion, and gave encouragement and admonition. They described their own experiences and testified to their present joys. They did not "take a text" or preach a sermon on a biblical passage. However, the exhorters often became the preachers when the circuit rider or pastor failed to show up.

Earlier in the Methodist movement, the Anglican Church frowned upon lay preaching. Susannah Wesley herself had alarmed her husband, an Anglican priest, by the "irregularity" of her fireside services. Her meetings were Bible studies and training sessions held in the rectory of Epworth.

John Wesley was finally forced to admit that laymen could do a more than an acceptable job of preaching, teaching, and ministry. Eventually he said, "Give me one hundred preachers who fear nothing but God, and I care not a straw whether they be clergymen or laymen, such alone will shake the gates of hell and set up the kingdom of heaven on earth."

Today, we need to remember our heritage and restore the ministry of the laity to become the Church as God intended it to be. Lay Speaking Ministries training equips laypersons to use their spiritual gifts for various kinds of ministry within the areas of leading, caring, and communicating. The experience, fellowship, and networking that occur in Lay Speaking Ministries and *Learning & Leading* courses prepare and encourage the laity in exploring the numerous types of mission and ministry opportunities. They cultivate a broader understanding of what it means to serve Christ both within and beyond the Church.

(For a brief history of Lay Speaking Ministries, see the last chapter of this book.)

Biblical Reflection

Read 1 Peter 2: 9-10.

1. What does it mean to you to be a member of Christ's royal priesthood?

2. How do you experience the priesthood of all believers in your life?

3. What mighty acts of God could you proclaim?

Notes

_____

_____

_____

_____

_____

_____

_____

_____

_____

_____

_____

_____

_____

_____

_____

_____

_____

_____

_____

Session Two

Leading

After he had washed their feet, had put on his robe and had returned to the table, he said to them, "Do you know what I have done to you? You call me Teacher and Lord—and you are right, for that is what I am. So if I, Your Lord and Teacher, have washed your feet, you also ought to wash one another's feet. For I have set you an example, that you also should do as I have done to you. Very truly, I tell you, servants are not greater than their master, nor are messengers greater than the one who sent them. If you know these things, you are blessed if you do them" (John 13:12-17).

Learning Outcome Goals

At the end of this session, the participant will be able to:

1. Describe servant leadership;
2. Discuss the important roles in leadership;
3. Describe and discuss what it means to be a spiritual leader;
4. Demonstrate the principles of Christian conferencing and describe consensus and discernment.

Servant Ministry

All Christians who are called to leadership are called to servant-hood. *The Book of Discipline* states in paragraphs 131 and 132 that the ministry of all Christians is one of service for the mission of God in the world. The teachings of Jesus on servant ministry and leadership shape this ministry. The United Methodist Church recognizes that God calls to leadership not only ordained clergy and deacons but also laypersons. Leadership helps form Christian disciples through spiritual formation and guidance for Christian living in the world.

Our ministry is both a privilege and an obligation. It is a privilege through our spiritual relationship with God to be a part of a holy nation, a royal priesthood, one of God's own people, and to proclaim the mighty acts of God (1 Peter 2:9).

The privilege of our spiritual relationship grows and transitions as we mature in our faith. This process requires intentional practice and nurture so that we may grow in grace (sanctifying grace) and move toward what John Wesley referred to as "Christian perfection." Wesley described perfection as a heart "habitually filled with the love of God and neighbor" and as "having the mind of Christ and walking as he walked."

> For the kingdom of God depends not on food and drink but righteousness and peace and joy in the Holy Spirit (Romans 14:17).

Servant ministry is also an obligation. The early Methodists developed a way of life that fostered reliability in their obligations to Jesus. General Rules (pages 71-74 of *The Book of Discipline*) express the methods of discipleship. John Wesley first published these rules in 1743, and they are still applicable today.

Servant Leadership

The call to servant leadership is a call experienced by lay and

Notes

ordained persons. This call is evidenced by special gifts, God's grace, and a promise of usefulness (*The Book of Discipline*, ¶136).

The privilege of servant leadership is the call to prepare the Church for mission in the world. The obligation or responsibility is the forming of Christian disciples and then guiding them in their witness. As servant leaders, we are inclusive by example as we serve all persons without discrimination. Marks of an inclusive society are "open, welcoming, fully accepting, and supporting" of all persons. This includes ensuring that settings for activities are accessible to persons with disabilities (*The Book of Discipline*, ¶138).

Jesus said, ". . . Whoever wishes to be great among you must be your servant" (Mt. 20:26). Jesus modeled servant leadership when he washed the disciples' feet.

Into the World

In Luke 10, we read of Jesus sending the seventy disciples in pairs to the places where he planned to visit. He told them how to reach people that they didn't know. He told them that the harvest was great and that the laborers were few. He also instructed them to pray for the Lord of the harvest and to ask him to send out more workers. When the disciples returned, they were amazed at what they were able to accomplish in Jesus' name. Jesus told them not to rejoice in the submission of the evil spirits but to rejoice that their names would be written in heaven.

Today, we must remember these principles as we begin our servant leadership. We prepare for this mission by studying with the Master. We must listen to the instructions he gives us and pray for help in all our endeavors. As we are in mission and ministry, we should not waste time in places where we are not welcome. And we should not be overly impressed by our accomplishments but be thankful that God has used us to help bring about God's kingdom.

As a servant leader, will you be able to delegate authority to those whom you serve? One way to check your leadership skills is to ask, "Are those being served growing in their faith and in their own skills as leaders?" An important aspect of servant leadership is encouraging others to grow and to use their spiritual gifts. Leaders who are spiritually immature or insecure can interfere with the growth of those whom they lead.

Principles of Christian Conferencing

- Inclusiveness
- Respectful Communication
- Guidelines
- Consensus and Discernment

Set a Spiritual Tone

- Focal point (candle, picture, etc.)
- Prayer
- Scripture
- Responsive Reading
- Songs

Beware of spiritual pride as a leader! Remember that Christians have equal access to God—our learning, our degrees, or our doctorates do not give us elite status in God's eyes. As we enter leadership positions, we must remain humble. And we must not serve out of our own motivations or to feed our own egos but with a motivation for the growth and well-being of others.

Your Role in Developing Leaders

One of the critical tasks of all leaders should be the development of future leaders. We should encourage and mentor others when

Notes

we see their potential for leadership. Be on the lookout for persons who exhibit leadership qualities. Encourage them to develop their spiritual gifts and to discover areas of passion in Christian ministry. Look for shining eyes—those who are excited about their roles in the priesthood of believers. Since none of us will be around forever, it is good stewardship to mentor others for leadership. The heart of leader development is having a vision beyond what you actually see when you look at someone believing in someone else even more than he believes in himself. It is to see beyond the actual to the potential, not just seeing who a person *is* but who she *can become*.

Magritte, a Belgian painter who lived in twentieth-century France, painted a great illustration of the heart of leadership development. His painting depicts a man seated in front of an almost completed painting of a bird. The man appears to be applying the finishing touches to his canvas. However, it is clear that the painter's inspiration isn't a bird but an egg. As he paints, he is looking beyond the egg to the bird, beyond the *actual* to the *potential*.

What did Jesus really have to work with? Not a whole lot! He chose a group of uneducated fishermen, a tax collector, and a couple of impetuous and potentially violent Jewish nationalists as his followers. If he had only looked at what was actual, there wasn't a whole lot to see: Peter, with his foot-in-mouth disease; Philip, who was timid and pessimistic; Thomas, who was continually doubtful and skeptical; James and John, full of selfish ambition.

Jesus had every reason to look away from each disciple if he had focused only on the actual, but he didn't. He looked beyond the actual to the potential. He put on the eyeglasses of potential, and each of the men (except one) went on to do great things for God.

For the apostle Paul, it was Barnabas who first believed in him. Paul mentored a number of men, including Timothy. When others saw a young leader who was often timid and perhaps not of as strong a personality as leadership would demand, Paul saw something much more and developed it. Paul eventually handed the baton of his ministry to Timothy.

Paul told Timothy to look out for other faithful men who could also teach others who could pass the baton of leadership down to the next generation. That baton has been passed from generation to generation all the way down to you. You are the one who is holding it now, and God gives you both the responsibility and the privilege to look for the next person to receive it from you as you pass it on.

The Means of Grace

- Worship
- Prayer
- Searching the Scriptures
- Lord's Supper
- Fasting or Abstinence
- Christian Conferencing
- Works of Mercy

Spiritual Leadership

As you therefore have received Christ Jesus the Lord, continue to live your lives in him, rooted and built up in him and established in the faith, just as you were taught, abounding in thanksgiving.

See to it that no one takes you captive through philosophy and empty deceit, according to human tradition, according to the elemental spirits of the universe, and not according to Christ (Colossians 2:6-8).

Be prepared spiritually for your role in leadership. Because you are a leader, others will look to you as a role model.

Notes

Notes

Spiritual Disciplines: A Call to Holy Living

> Therefore prepare your minds for action; discipline yourselves; set all your hope on the grace that Jesus Christ will bring you when he is revealed. Like obedient children, do not be conformed to the desires that you formerly had in ignorance. Instead, as he who called you is holy, be holy yourselves in all your conduct; for it is written, "You shall be holy for I am holy" (1 Peter 1:13-15).

Wesley called these spiritual disciplines the means of grace and the "ordinances of God." These are the practices, or means, of staying in relationship with God. The practice of the means of grace enables Christians to obey the command to love God with all their hearts, and with all their souls and with all their strength and with all their minds, to love their neighbors as themselves and to love one another as Christ loves. When Christians make these means of grace habits in their daily lives, they will grow in holiness of heart and life.

The key to Christian growth is not feeling but faithfulness. If believers left it up to feelings, there would be and probably are days that they would not "feel" like praying or searching scripture. Faithfulness calls all believers to these means of grace, whether they feel like it or not! God is faithful in providing these means of grace and Christians must be faithful in practicing them.

Look at your spiritual practices, cultivate new ones, and grow in your faith. Make these practices a part of who you are, and model these practices in your church, at meetings, and within your families. Encourage team participants to practice spiritual disciplines and to grow in their relationships with God.

In the Wesley societies and class meetings, there were rules to be followed. There were expectations for membership, and people were held accountable for following these rules.

Wesley's view of these rules was that they were not church law but a way of discipleship. These rules were restated by Rueben Job in *Three Simple Rules* (Abingdon Press).

The General Rule maintains balance between all of the teachings of Jesus.

The General Rules

It is therefore expected of all who continue therein that they should continue to evidence their desire for salvation

First: By doing no harm, by avoiding evil of every kind . . .

Secondly: By doing good; by being in every kind merciful after their power; as they have opportunity, doing good of every possible sort . . .

Thirdly: By attending upon all the ordinances of God . . . (*The Book of Discipline* ¶103).

THE GENERAL RULE OF DISCIPLESHIP

To witness to Jesus Christ in the world, and to follow his teachings through acts of compassion, justice, worship, and devotion under the guidance of the Holy Spirit.

Notes

Notes

Accountable/Covenant Discipleship

Covenant Discipleship groups are designed to function as the Wesley class meetings. Many churches have developed small groups for fellowship and study, but they are not designed to hold members accountable for their spiritual growth.

The General Rules suggest that Christ's life and teachings compel his disciples toward a balance between works of mercy (compassion and justice) and works of piety (worship and devotion). These acts are both private (as the acts of compassion and devotion) and public (acts of justice and worship). Acts of compassion are the actions we take to meet the needs of our neighbor, who is anyone we encounter in need. Acts of justice are related because that is when we ask the "what" and "why." *Why is our neighbor suffering? What is the cause?*

Acts of devotion are the means of grace we practice to care for our relationship with God. They include prayer, fasting, and journaling, and they help us center our daily lives in Christ.

Acts of worship are the public giving of ourselves to God and includes the place where Christians come to praise, sing, pray, and hear the Word proclaimed.

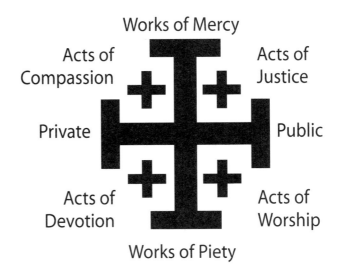

Works of Mercy

Acts of Compassion — Acts of Justice

Private — Public

Acts of Devotion — Acts of Worship

Works of Piety

Covenant Discipleship groups are meetings where Christians "watch over one another in love" by giving each other a weekly checkup in discipleship. They are gatherings of people whose task is to help one another become better disciples. One of the most important dynamics of a Covenant Discipleship (CD) group is the relationship formed between the members of the group. Covenant Discipleship groups are trustworthy and an effective means of identifying and nurturing leaders in discipleship for mission and ministry. They are not where our discipleship happens, but where we make sure that it happens.

Leaders who are disciples are called to witness to Christ in the world by following his teachings. We live the story by making his teachings, his life, and his commandments part of our lives. Disciplined leaders bring good news to the poor, release to the captives, open the eyes of the blind, and liberate the oppressed. They feed the hungry, give drink to the thirsty, clothe the naked, welcome the stranger, care for the homeless, and visit the sick and imprisoned. Disciplined leaders love God and their neighbors as themselves. They love one another as Christ loves them, and they forgive as Christ forgives.

Perfection

- Singleness of intention
- Power over sin
- Radical dependence on Christ
- Equipment for ministry
- An experience to grow in

The United Methodist Church holds that the work of salvation—God's acceptance and pardon—in spite of our sin, does not end with our being forgiven. The saving work of God continues to nurture us and to allow us to grow in grace. The power of the Holy Spirit enables us to grow in the knowledge of love of God and neighbor.

Notes

35

Notes

This increasing in love and knowledge is called sanctifying grace, and it draws us toward the gift that John Wesley called Christian perfection. Wesley described Christian perfection as a heart filled with the love of God and neighbor.

Christian perfection does not mean spiritual infallibility, nor does it mean that one is a superior Christian. It means holiness, and it is not static or a one-time experience. It is singleness of purpose, a desire to do God's will and to discover a central purpose. It is our controlling desire to do God's will on earth as it is in heaven. God knows our intentions, and when it is our intention to live in God's will, then God calls it perfect, even though it may include some weeds and dirt. In other words, God does not negate the relationship when the performance is flawed.

Leadership Tools

As a leader, certain tools can help you plan, organize, and set goals for projects, missions, and ministries.

Discover Current Reality

The current reality is "the way things are right now." Now is the time to gather information about the state of the affairs regarding your project and the church. Here is a chance to practice listening to God's voice regarding your area of ministry and taking notes on important facts that will affect your planning. Look at your role and place in a faithful community that extends itself in mission by reaching out and receiving people, relating people to God, nurturing them in Christ and Christian living, and sending them forth as ministers in the world.

Name Shared Vision

How does God envision the mission and ministry of your church? Spend some time with church committees and leaders to

36

discern the best future for the mission or ministry. Look at the big picture and try to see yourselves as God's agents of grace and love. When you share a vision, it gains support and power. It is worth the time it will take to get all participants of the same mind so that they can work together toward a common goal.

DEVELOP ACTION PLANS

Your action plans are the ways to get from current reality to shared vision. As a leader, one of your tasks is to hold both what is and what is hoped for in view so that you can build bridges for the future. The bridges are the interim goals and action plans needed to make the vision a reality.

Be flexible because God may open different avenues than what you have planned. Remember that action plans should be specific, measurable, and attainable. Place your plans in God's hands. Faithful leaders are attentive to the discernment of the congregation and team members and to the heart of God in fulfilling the mission of the church. Planning and praying together help keep everyone focused on the goal or vision.

MONITOR THE JOURNEY

Keep an eye on how things are going, and do your best to keep moving in spite of setbacks. Accept setbacks as inevitable, and don't be surprised because they will occur. Satan will surely attempt to thwart any plans to grow the kingdom of God. Evaluate accomplishments in light of the ministry of the rest of the church or community. Keep your mission in line with God's mission by honest evaluation and discernment of the effectiveness or impact of the mission or ministry project.

UNITY OF MINISTRY

The Book of Discipline talks about the call of all Christians through their baptism to share God's love in the world. There are those

Notes

Notes

called to servant leadership, both lay and ordained. Such callings are evidenced by special gifts and the presence of God's grace. Each Christian has the promise of usefulness for spreading the Good News and making disciples.

Paragraph 129 of *The Book of Discipline* discusses the unity of ministry in Christ. It says:

> There is but one ministry in Christ, but there are diverse gifts and evidences of God's grace in the body of Christ (Ephesians 4:4-16). The ministry of *all* [emphasis by author] Christians is complementary. No ministry is subservient to another. All United Methodists are summoned and sent by Christ to live and work together in mutual interdependence and to be guided by the Spirit into the truth that frees and the love that reconciles.

All roles are important in the church, and none is subservient or less important than another. Laity and clergy, preachers and lay speakers, are all partners in ministry, working together to make disciples for Jesus Christ.

There are diverse spiritual gifts, and no one person has them all. No pastor, no matter how wonderful, can possibly do all the ministry. That's why we are the Body of Christ—we have gifts that differ, none more important than the other. Ephesians 4:11-13 tells us that some are called to be apostles, prophets, evangelists, pastors, and teachers to prepare God's people for works of service so that the Body of Christ may be built up until we all reach unity in the faith. Verse 16 goes on to say, ". . . from whom [Christ] the whole body, joined and held together by every ligament with which it is equipped, as each part is working properly, promotes the body's growth in building itself up in love."

As laity in leadership, we must find ways to foster and expand the ministry of all Christians. As laity serve with clergy, it is important that we exhibit mutual advocacy. We must stand up for each other and encourage those who have problems to seek conversation and reconciliation. Part of working together is to encourage one another by providing constructive feedback and giving support. Good communication must be developed so that we can interpret actions and build trust. Being honest and trustworthy is essential to developing a working partnership. It is helpful to attempt to understand differences in personalities, age, and experiences to build relationships. Pray for each other regularly. As trust develops, share prayer concerns. Regardless of who initiates it, both parties should work toward a trusting relationship and shared responsibilities. The church will be more effective in all that it does when all of the people of God are using their gifts in ministry and mission.

Leading Meetings

One role of leadership is leading meetings. It is important to plan meetings so that they can be as productive as possible. No one likes to attend meetings that are disorganized and unfruitful.

Christian Conferencing

The practice of holy conferencing is the manner in which we govern our lives together. This practice can profoundly affect our church because it calls us to build each other up—not tear each other down—and it emphasizes fellowship within the Body of Christ.

All meetings should be times of Christian or holy conferencing. If we tithe our meeting time, then we should spend one tenth of every meeting in devotions and prayer. When we lead meetings with "bookend" prayers, we miss the opportunity to truly fellowship and form community. We must remember whose work we are doing when we meet. *Whose church is this?* It is God's.

Try lighting a Christ candle, having a sacred picture in view,

Notes

Notes

or keeping an empty chair for Jesus to remind yourselves of the presence of Christ with you. Set the tone of the meeting by meditating on scripture and praying over personal and meeting agenda concerns. Lifting prayer concerns at the beginning of the meeting and giving them to God can help participants focus on the work at hand. Make each meeting a spiritual gathering.

Plan the agenda to include time for this spiritual nurture, and allow time for prayer and discernment over decisions the group makes. It will not take more time, and by setting a spiritual tone for the meeting, you will affect the mood of those gathered.

Practice inclusiveness when forming committees or work-groups. Make sure that meeting places are handicap-accessible. Provide childcare. Do your best to provide a welcoming atmosphere for all involved. Set up communication guidelines for all meetings. (See session five for more on respectful communication guidelines.)

DISCERNMENT

Discernment is simply looking for God's guidance in a situation. It means listening for God's voice and seeking direction as you make plans for the work of mission and ministry. When you use discernment you are trying to see to the heart of the matter with spiritual eyes.

> And when you turn to the right or when you turn to the left, your ears shall hear a word behind you, saying, "This is the way; walk in it" (Is. 30:21).

Discernment is not a new concept! Samuel listened to God's voice to discern which of Jesse's sons would be anointed king. Solomon requested a wise and discerning mind. Romans 12:2 says, "Be transformed by the renewing of your mind so that you may **discern** what is the will of God—what is good and acceptable and perfect."

1 Cor. 12:10 speaks of the spiritual gift of discernment

between spirits, and 1 John 4:1 says, ". . . Do not believe every spirit, but test [discern] the spirits to see whether they are from God." Because early Christians feared the voices of false prophets, they "tested" the spirits. The Spirit of God determined what served the common good of the community. Remember the argument in Acts about whether new converts needed to be circumcised? The apostles and elders met to consider the question, and they came to one mind and heart through discernment (Acts 15).

The purpose and goal of spiritual discernment is knowing and doing God's will. We must keep our eyes and our hearts on that purpose and goal. Why, with this long history of the use of discernment, do we ignore it in our church decision making today? Be sure to take time for prayer and discernment when making any decisions regarding your mission and ministries.

A Process for Discernment

Framing: Clearly state the question, the subject of the discernment.

Grounding: Select and state guiding principles, beliefs, and values that the group may revisit at any point in the discernment process.

Shedding: Bring prejudices, false assumptions, predetermined desires or conclusions, and ego defenses or concerns to light and lay them aside. This is the "letting go" and "opening up" process.

Rooting: Relate the subject in question to biblical images, texts, and stories of your own religious tradition.

Listening: This involves everything from silent prayer, to conducting research, to asking others and sharing experiences. It is one of the central steps.

Exploring: Use the power of imagination to identify all the possible directions or options, and

Notes

41

Notes

examine them in the light of the grounding principles.

Improving: Select the best possible options from the exploring segment and improve or flesh them out so the group can articulate them well.

Weighing: Select options based on the preferences of the group. Test using practical judgment, through reason, intuition, and tradition (rooting).

Closing: Close the discussion and establish the decision or direction. Gather consensus.

Resting: Allow the decision to rest to see whether it brings a sense of peace and movement toward God or a sense of distress and movement away from God (Chuck Olsen and Danny Morris, *Discerning God's Will Together* [Upper Room Books]).

CONSENSUS

Consensus means a general agreement or harmony among a group of people. When there is consensus among the members of a group, it creates a cooperative dynamic. The people work together for the best possible decision for the group.

Somewhere along the way, the church has come to use a secular model, *Robert's Rules of Order*, for governing itself. We have lost the focus on discernment and consensus and use parliamentary procedure to conduct our meetings. Other churches, like the Quakers and the Uniting Church of Australia, have concluded that consensus is a better format for making decisions.

In parliamentary procedure, we employ motions, amendments, and amendments of amendments until we vote. Often, this process results in a division of the body and produces a win/lose situation. If the presider is not an expert with the procedures, mass confusion can result. It is just as acceptable to attack and diminish another's point of view as it is to promote and endorse your own ideas. Voting can happen without a clear picture of the issue because of the adversarial environment.

With the consensus model, however, decision-makers hear and understand every interest, and everyone accepts the outcome. They all don't necessarily agree, but they do agree to set disagreement aside so that the group can reach an agreement (consensus). The group accepts the decision even though not all its members may agree. This happens because all members believe the group heard them and considered their needs and concerns.

In consensus, everyone seeks an alternative that addresses all concerns and interests. Members seek something greater, a higher ground that surpasses anyone's preconceived ideas of what the decision should be. With consensus, there is an obligation not to stymie the group or decision but to help the group meet everyone's interests and needs. And there is an obligation to continue to try to meet the interests and needs of those who stand aside. There is group ownership of the decision, fostering cooperation, an attitudes which may not occur in win/lose situations.

As a leader, you will have an opportunity to change the status quo and to make a difference- in how your church holds meetings and forms community through the promotion of Christian conferencing, the process of discernment and consensus forming.

Biblical Reflection

> After he had washed their feet, had put on his robe, and had returned to the table, he said to them, "Do you know what I have done for you? You call me Teacher and Lord—and you are right, for that is what I am. So if I, your Lord and Teacher, have washed your feet, you also ought to wash one another's feet. For I have set you an example, that you also should do as I

Notes

Notes

have done to you. Very truly, I tell you, servants are not greater than their master, nor are messengers greater than the one who sent them. If you know these things, you are blessed if you do them" (John 13:12-17).

1. Who has served as an example of servant leader for you?

2. How did this person exhibit servant leadership?

3. How can you serve and lead at the same time?

4. Why is servant leadership important?

Session Three

Caring

" . . . For I was hungry and you gave me food, I was thirsty and you gave me something to drink, I was a stranger and you welcomed me, I was naked and you gave me clothing, I was sick and you took care of me, I was in prison and you visited me." . . . And the king will answer them, "Truly I tell you, just as you did it to one of the least of these who are members of my family, you did it to me" (Matthew 25: 35-37, 40).

Learning Outcome Goals

At the end of this session, the participant will be able to:

1. Discuss the biblical basis for caring ministry;
2. Compare and contrast acts of compassion and acts of justice;
3. Discuss several types of caring ministries;
4. Discuss ways to show care for creation.

Notes

Every Person Needs

Security	Safety
Touch	Belonging
Significance	Grieving
Attention	Sexuality
Guidance	Accomplishment
Support	Nurturing
Freedom	Trust

Caring is an essential part of all ministry and leadership. Jesus said that the greatest commandment was to "love God with all your heart, soul, and mind, and the second is to love your neighbor as yourself." In a society that tends to put "me" first, this is difficult. However, when we apply caring principles to everything we do and increase our awareness of ways to show care and compassion, caring will become easier.

Every person has needs beyond the basics of food and shelter. They are security, safety, touch, belonging, significance, grieving, attention, sexuality, guidance, accomplishment, support, nurturing, freedom, and trust. In addition, every person has feelings in varying degrees, including hurt, loneliness, sadness, fear, shame, guilt, gladness, anger. Knowing this should help us as we relate to others because we know that we all share these basic needs and emotions. Caring for others comes more naturally to some people than others, but all people can work to understand, love and care for their neighbors. Who is our neighbor? Everyone!

Responding to the Needs of the World

Christians in ministry can find are endless ways of responding to the hurts and needs of the world. They range from serving as a missionary in a foreign country to listening to the concerns of a friend or co-worker. When we discern our call and discover our spiritual gifts, the specific ways we can care for our neighbors may become clearer.

Serving in missions, whether short term or long, in your community, across the nation, or beyond our borders, is a way to respond. When we use our gifts and abilities to serve others outside of our family or circle of friends, even in our congregation, we are in mission. There are many opportunities through Volunteers in Mission, our annual conferences or districts, and community organizations to provide help to those in need.

Works of Mercy: Types of Caring Ministries

Caring ministries come in all sorts of programs and service opportunities. Finding our niche can take some time because not only are we not all gifted the same, but we do not all have the same passions. Be patient, look to see where God is at work, and join God in that work. Do you have a passion for prayer, for homeless or prison ministry? Check out the programs in your area where you can explore ways to care for others in these areas.

PRAYER MINISTRY

Prayer is an action; it is doing something. Too often, we tend to think that by praying for someone or for a situation we are not really doing anything. Sometimes prayer is the only thing we can do or the best thing we can do! If we are gifted with the spiritual gift of intercession, then prayer may be the perfect way for us to care for others. Even if we do not have that particular gift, we may have a passion for prayer and find fulfillment in the command to love others through prayer.

Notes

Notes

PRISON MINISTRY

> Remember those who are in prison, as though you were in prison with them (Hebrews 13:3).

John Wesley defined true religion as love for God and neighbor, and he considered friendship and visiting with the poor an essential part of discipleship. In fact, it was just as important to Wesley to visit the sick and imprisoned as it was to pray or partake in Holy Communion. Therefore, prison ministry is not an option for United Methodists if we are to be followers of Jesus. Not everyone will feel comfortable visiting a prison, so once again this is a time to consider gifts and passion. But we must be careful not to dismiss the mandatory nature of this ministry by using excuses to avoid doing it. If we are not actually participating in the ministry, then we must find ways to support those who are. We may be in the position to employ a former prisoner or support the families of prisoners.

The 1996 General Conference added to the Social Principles a statement regarding restorative justice ministries that states, "In the love of Christ, who came to save those who are lost and vulnerable, we urge the creation of genuinely new systems for the care and support of the victims of crime and for rehabilitation that will restore, preserve, and nurture the humanity of the imprisoned" (Social Principles, 68.F).

There are many ways to put our faith into action, and the church must understand the need for ministry to the imprisoned, to victims of crime, to their families and to the community. We must strive to heal those who have been wounded and to work for the transformation of those who have inflicted the wounds.

Kairos is an organization of ministries that address the spiritual needs of incarcerated men, women, and children, their families, and those who work in the prison environment. The mission of the Kairos Prison Ministry is to bring Christ's love and forgiveness to all incarcerated individuals, their families, and those who work with them, and to assist in the transition toward becoming productive citizens. This particular ministry sprang from the Cursillo movement and The Upper Room Walk to Emmaus. These programs are for both men and women and are a three-day weekend programs best described as "short courses in Christianity." Both The General Board of Global Ministries and The General Board of Church and Society of the United Methodist Church work with prison ministry concerns.

STEPHEN MINISTRY

Stephen Ministry is a ministry of caring which provides one-to-one Christian care to hurting people. *Care givers* (Stephen Ministers) are paired with *care receivers* who are the bereaved, hospitalized, terminally ill, separated, divorced, unemployed, relocated, or facing another crisis or life challenge. A Stephen Minister provides care by listening and giving support to an individual. The care giver and care receiver meet regularly, usually once a week at the beginning of their relationship, and the care giver attends supervision meetings with other care givers to gain wisdom and guidance for care giving. All interactions and discussions are confidential. There is a specific training program for Stephen Ministry and resources available to set up a Stephen Ministry program in any congregation.

Acts of Compassion

In session two, we talked about accountable or covenant discipleship and acts of compassion. Acts of compassion are anything one does to demonstrate love of God by caring for creation and neighbor. Acts of compassion show our care for others, but they require us to move beyond the feeling and verbalization of care to actual demonstrations of it.

These compassionate actions range from coming to the aid of a stranger or calling a shut-in to planting a tree, from praying

Notes

Notes

with someone to recycling, from giving someone physical aid to feeding the birds. Acts of compassion are more than random acts of kindness; they are intentional ways that we demonstrate God's love to others. We become Christ for others when we do things that Christ would do. Jesus didn't just talk about healing, he did it. He didn't just talk about feeding the people; he fed people.

> "A man was going down from Jerusalem to Jericho, and fell into the hands of robbers, who stripped him, beat him and went away, leaving him half dead. . . . A Samaritan while traveling came near him; and when he saw him, he was moved with pity. He went to him and bandaged his wounds, having poured oil and wine on them. Then he put him on his own animal, brought him to an inn and took care of him" (Luke 10:30, 33-34).

Acts of Justice

Acts of justice are another part of balanced or holistic discipleship. We participate in acts of justice when we seek to remedy the cause of homelessness, poverty, debilitating diseases, crime, or war. These actions to correct injustices can range from praying for peace to writing a member of congress about an important bill to improve education for the poor; from making sure you welcome strangers to providing funding for organizations who work for peace and justice; from being inclusive in committees and work groups to signing petitions and joining protest demonstrations for equal rights. There are many ways to show our care for others. Acts of justice differ from acts of compassion because they are actions that work to fix the cause of unfair the situations. Acts of compassion without acts of justice are like putting a bandage on a gaping wound. We need to eliminate the cause of the illness, the poverty, or the hunger.

The Social Principles address many of the issues for which the United Methodist Church has concern. Take some time to read the resolutions for a better understanding of the issues and visit the website of the General Board of Church and Society (www.gbcs.org) to discover ways of resolving these various concerns.

RACIAL/ETHNIC/CULTURAL CARES

One of the major concerns in our society and in our churches is the practice of inclusiveness. Working to ensure justice and inclusiveness is one way of showing care or love for our neighbor. Remember our neighbor is everyone, even Samaritans. For some reason, we have problems accepting others who may be different from us. We often hold them suspect and do not trust them. Therefore, we do not make an effort to accept them into our churches, communities, or families. They may act differently, look differently, or even smell differently, so we are unwilling to have them become a part of our group. When we fail to do this, we forget that God created diversity. Look at all the different flowers, trees, and animals, that there are. We marvel at that diversity while we reject human diversity. As a leader in the church, it is vitally important that we are willing to accept diversity, treat all persons equally, and work for inclusiveness.

LISTENING

Sometimes the most important thing we can do to care for our neighbor is to listen. Like prayer, listening can feel like we aren't *doing* anything. But like prayer, listening is essential to all forms of caring.

Listening may provide the key to what action someone needs. Has the listening ear ever been a blessing to someone in distress? Yes, but listening is hard to do. We want to provide the answers, we want to make it all better, and we want to fix it.

Notes

Notes

However, many times the best fix is to listen and allow the emptying of words from the other. Listening is a critical part of communication.

THE MINISTRY OF PRESENCE

At times when there is nothing to do but be *present* with someone. To be at someone's side may be the most caring thing we can do. After mission trips or other forms of mission and ministry, we may wonder what we did to make a difference or what we actually accomplished. Our presence was an accomplishment; it makes a difference to those who feel no one cares. Our presence shows that we care enough to leave the demands of our personal lives to spend time with those in need.

Caring Responses

As we listen and care for others, we need to maintain a non-judgmental attitude. Remember that Jesus said, "Let anyone among you who is without sin be the first to throw a stone at her" (John 8:7). We need to keep our tendency to judge others in check in order to care for them.

It is important to create a safe and supportive environment when we are listening and present with others. They will not be comfortable sharing if we do not establish an atmosphere of trust. Our role as leaders is to help those whom we lead understand and practice this attitude. We can do this best by setting an example.

Caring for Creation

> The LORD God took the man and put him in the garden to till it and keep it (Genesis 2:15).

God created humankind to care for the earth. That is the

purpose of our existence, to care for God's creation—humans, animals, plants, the ground, the seas, and the atmosphere. We are

> We do not inherit the Earth from our ancestors; we borrow it from our children (Ancient Indian Proverb).

called to be stewards of all that God has given us.

We must be aware of the things that we do that harm the earth and its inhabitants. We must work to correct our actions and restore the health of our world.

"The earth is the LORD'S and all that is in it, the world and those who live in it" (Ps. 24:1). We cannot take our planet for granted. The beauty and balance of our environment is our responsibility. Caring for the environment and the ecosystems of our planet demonstrates a caring attitude toward others and an appreciation for the gifts of God.

Find ways to become involved in the care of the world and encourage others to do the same. As a leader and a Christian, this is a part of your responsibility.

Caring Skills

> Let the same mind be in you that was in Christ Jesus (Philippians 2:5).

In order to lead in a ministry of caring we must be spiritually prepared. In Romans Paul tells us to ". . . be transformed by the renewing of *our* minds so that *we* may discern what is the will of God—what is good and acceptable and perfect"(Romans 12:2, italics added).

We must practice listening to God and to others to discern what to do to care for others and for creation. And we must be prepared to provide appropriate verbal responses as we listen to

Notes

Notes

others who may object to our mission of caring and to those for whom we are caring. One way to accomplish this is to spend time in prayer, not only speaking to God, but also taking time to listen —to be still and know.

". . . If my people, who are called by my name, will humbles themselves, pray, seek my face, and turn from their wicked ways, then I will hear from heaven, and will forgive their sin and heal their land" (2 Chronicles 7:14).

Biblical Reflection

". . . For I was hungry and you gave me food, I was thirsty and you gave me something to drink, I was a stranger and you welcomed me, I was naked and you gave me clothing, I was sick and you took care of me, I was in prison and you visited me." . . . And the king will answer them, "Truly I tell you, just as you did it to one of the least of these who are members of my family, you did it to me" (Matthew 25: 35-37, 40).

Read Matthew 25:31-46.

1. After reading Matthew 25:31-46, describe ways God judges the nations.

2. In what ways do you evidence your belief in Jesus Christ by caring for the hungry, thirsty, strangers, naked, sick, and imprisoned?

3. What opportunities have you experienced and neglected to act upon to care for your neighbors?

4. In what specific ways can you improve your caring responses to your neighbors?

Session Four

Communicating

But how are they to call on one in whom they have not believed? And how are they to believe in one of whom they have never heard? And how are they to hear without someone to proclaim him? And how are they to proclaim him unless they are sent? As it is written, "How beautiful are the feet of those who bring good news!" . . . So faith comes from what is heard, and what is heard comes through the word of Christ (Romans 10:14-15, 17).

Learning Outcome Goals

At the end of this session the participant will be able to:

1. Discuss the importance of communication skills;
2. List the Respectful Communication Guidelines;
3. Describe the process of mutual invitation;
4. Demonstrate listening skills;
5. Share a faith story with another participant.

Notes

The Importance and Impact of Communication

We hear a lot about communication, and we have amazing technology to help us communicate. And yet, we still suffer from a lack of communication! We know that in order for information to be transmitted, it must get from the source to the receiver. But there are so many obstacles that can get in the way and block the transmission. In this session we are going to talk a bit about communication skills and why they are important in sharing information and our faith stories.

One of the most important pieces of information that we must communicate as Christians is the Good News. How will our neighbors or loved ones hear if we don't tell them? One of our responsibilities as Christian leaders is to communicate not only information regarding leadership or discipleship but also the Good News of God's saving grace through Jesus Christ. This does not mean standing on a street corner shouting for people to repent and sin no more, nor does it mean quoting scripture to folks. It means sharing from your heart your faith story with those with whom you have a relationship. Perhaps a relative, neighbor, or co-worker notices that you have a great amount of faith or are able to handle stress, difficulties, or anger with quiet strength. They may ask you how you are able to do that or why you are different. That is an open invitation to share the reason for the hope that lies within you.

Also as leaders, we must be able to communicate to those whom we lead. Communication is a way to plant ideas clearly, and people are more likely to listen to and have confidence in a leader who is a good communicator.

Good communication requires two skills: the skill of speaking and the skill of listening. Communication involves what we intend to say, what we actually say, the message the listeners hear, the listeners' responses, and our reactions to their responses! No wonder things can get misinterpreted! In our speaking we give feedback that includes the expression of our feelings, sharing of information and ideas, demonstrating an understanding of the other person(s), and making observations.

Communication Settings

PERSON TO PERSON

Communicating person-to-person or one-on-one is probably one of the most important communication settings. And yet it is probably the one we prepare for the least. In all communications it is important to speak with a purpose rather than rambling. Because whining or pleading does not instill respect or interest in what we have to say, we must be sure to modulate our voices to avoid sounding as though we are complaining or urging. If the conversation becomes upsetting, it is best to request to be excused to continue the discussion after there has been a chance to think things through and we are able to speak calmly.

PERSONAL SPACE

Do not intrude on a person's personal space. It is uncomfortable to have someone "in your face," so to speak. Retain a respectful distance. If the one-on-one meeting is with someone of the opposite gender, be sure to meet in a place where the integrity of both individuals will not be questioned.

MUTUAL UNDERSTANDING

Understanding others and our own self-awareness promotes mutual understanding. A tool developed in the 1950s that can help us assess and improve individual and group relationships is called the Johari Window.

Notes

Notes

JOHARI WINDOW	
1 open/free area	2 blind area
3 hidden area	4 unknown area

The Johari Window represents information, including feelings, experiences, views, attitudes, skills, intentions, motivation, etc., within or about a person from four perspectives. Each of the four areas represents information about a person and whether that information is known or unknown by the person or by others in a group.

- Area 1 represents what is known by the person and is also known by others.
- Area 2 represents what is unknown by the person about him/herself but which others know, hence the term "blind" area.
- Area 3 represents what the person knows about him/herself that others do not know, or the "hidden" area.
- Area 4 represents what is unknown to the person about him/herselves and is also unknown by others in a group.

These areas or window panes can change in size to reflect the proportion of knowledge in that area. For instance in new relationships or groups the "open or free" space is small because not much has been shared. But as the person becomes better known in the relationship or group, the window enlarges.

The aim in good communication is to develop or enlarge area 1, indicating openness, trust, and understanding.

When people increase their "open" area, their area 2 or blind area (known to others but unknown to self) can shrink as there is feedback from others and increased self-awareness.

The hidden area can include fears, sensitivities, hidden agendas, and manipulative intentions, etc., which are known to the person but not to others. When self-disclosure reduces this area, the "open" area increases, and the hidden area decreases.

Area 4 contains information, feelings, latent abilities, aptitudes, and experiences that are unknown to the person and to others. These can be the deeper aspects of our personalities that may influence our behavior. These unknown traits or talents can be revealed through self-discovery or observation by others. For instance, someone may not realize that he or she has a certain spiritual gift until another person discovers or recognizes that previously unknown gift.

All of this is to say that as we develop relationships through good communication skills, we can observe the changes in the areas of the Johari Window in people with whom we communicate. It is important to realize that these areas exist in each of us. Leaders can help create an environment that fosters trust and openness, encouragement, and self-discovery.

Special Situations

Non–Native Language

Here are a few things to remember when communicating with people for whom English is not their primary language.

Speak clearly, pronounce words correctly, but not loudly. They don't have a hearing problem; their primary language is not your primary language.

Do not cover your mouth when you talk.

Avoid running words together. (*Djoueatjet? Nodjou?*)

Notes

Notes

Use simple words and avoid colloquialisms. (*Way cool, gotcha', or totally.*)

Do not show frustration at their lack of understanding. Smile and wait for questions of clarification. Remember that your particular dialect may not be the way they heard the language when they learned it. (*Ya'll, Youn's, Yinz.*)

Say *yes* or *no*, not *uh-huh* or *uh-uh*. Be careful shaking your head—in some cultures, shaking your head *yes* (for Americans) actually means *no*.

Try communicating a concept by drawing or by writing the word on paper. People may understand visually rather than by the spoken word, especially if you have a regional accent.

COMMUNICATING WITH OTHER AGE GROUPS

Keep in mind as you speak to younger people, remember that you were that age at one time. And for older people that you may be that age one day! We should respect whatever is on anyone's mind, regardless of his or her age.

- Avoid responding in a condescending manner. Do not make people feel as if they are stupid.
- Avoid preaching or nagging.
- Do not try to be cool or say you understand when you may not have had their experiences.

MENTALLY-CHALLENGED PERSONS

Communicating with those whose speech is limited by mental deficiency is a skill that one can develop. Because each person should be treated with dignity, it is important to understand that they have some different needs:

- Maintain a calm, low volume.
- Speak to their mental age, not chronological age.
- Do not mimic their pronunciation of words.
- Use simple words and do not run them together.

- Look them in the eye and communicate a caring attitude. Patiently listen.
- Smile to let them know you appreciate them.
- Beware of a patronizing tone in your voice.

Practice the Golden Rule in communication and speak to others in ways in which you would like to be spoken. Demonstrate respect and care in your communications.

Small Groups

Most researchers define a small group as having at least three and no more than fifteen members. These groups could be committees, classes, or other workgroups. A group must have a common purpose or goal, and its members must work together to achieve that goal. The goal brings the group together and holds it together through conflict and tension.

A group's members must be able to communicate freely and openly with all of the other members of the group. Groups will develop ways of discussing their work, and group members will develop roles that they fill within the group that will affect the group's interaction and relationships.

Consideration for All

One of the most important things to remember in small-group communication is that all members should be treated well. Encourage everyone to participate, and respect each as individuals. This may mean that some members must be "drawn out" while others may need to be "stifled." Consideration also means that the leader must prepare for the meeting, showing respect for the group's time.

Preparation

Being prepared for small-group meetings of all kinds is essential.

Notes

Whether you are leading a committee meeting or teaching a class, the process will go much better when you plan ahead. As we plan for this small-group time, focus on God's plan for this time together and the purpose of the meeting. Stay open to the Holy Spirit's guidance. Plan what will happen to make this a time of holy conferencing. Set goals with the group so that all members know what the group intends to accomplish. Prepare an agenda if it is appropriate and distribute it before the meeting, if possible.

PRACTICE RESPECTFUL COMMUNICATION

Follow the guidelines for respectful communication. These guidelines may even be posted in your meeting room, and each group member should be given a copy. A covenant can be formed within the group to follow these guidelines at all gatherings of the group.

Respectful Communications Guidelines

R = take Responsibility for what you say and feel, without blaming others.

E = Empathetic listening. Try to understand how the other person feels.

S = be Sensitive to differences in communication styles.

P = Ponder on what you hear and feel before you speak.

E = Examine your own assumptions and perceptions.

C = keep Confidential what others have to say.

T = Tolerate what others have to say.

(Copyright Eric Law. Used by permission.)

MUTUAL INVITATION

Use the mutual invitation process to provide an opportunity for everyone to speak. It is a way to control people who tend to dominate meetings and give those who are quiet a chance to speak.

This is the process: The leader may take a "talking piece" (an object that can be held in the hands, e.g., a small cross or a small stone) and hand it to a person who is invited to speak. The "talking piece" serves as a reminder that all others are quiet while the person holding the talking piece is speaking.

The invited person may choose to speak or may pass. If the person chooses to speak, then he or she hands the "talking piece" to another group member when he or she finishes. If the person chooses to pass, he or she may simply hand the "talking piece" to another member as a signal to speak.

Another way to do this is to place the "talking piece" in a central location and those who choose to speak may pick it up, speak, and then replace it for another person to use. This method may not work as well when we attempt to give quiet group members a chance to speak.

LISTENING

Not many people master the skill of listening. However, listening is a skill we can always improve. Holding one's tongue can be a challenge on our best days. But true listening is more than holding our tongues. Listening is suspending our own agendas and immersing ourselves in what the other person is saying. Listening and being listened to are basic ways that we acknowledge and recognize one another as sharing a common humanity. Through listening, we experience communion. Community cannot exist where people are unable or unwilling to listen to each other.

Good listening is an *active* part of communication and one of the most important skills we can have. How well we listen has a major impact on our relationships and communication effectiveness. We listen for many reasons including to obtain information,

Notes

Notes

to understand, for enjoyment, and to learn. It has been said that we remember between twenty-five and fifty percent of what we hear. We may not think of it as being an activity, but listening requires as much if not more attention and action than speaking. By becoming better listeners, we will improve our abilities as communicators to influence people and decrease the number of conflicts and misunderstandings in our relationships.

Active listening requires a conscious effort to hear the words other people say and, more importantly, to understand the message they are trying to convey. The following are some key points for active listening.

Pay attention:

- Look at the speaker, and make eye contact;
- Put aside distracting thoughts. Don't think about what you will say in response;
- Avoid being distracted by the surroundings;
- "Listen" to the speaker's body language.

Show that you are listening:

- Nod occasionally;
- Smile or use other facial expressions;
- Note your body language. It should indicate openness;
- Do not interrupt, but encourage the speaker with small verbal comments like *yes* or *uh-huh*.

Provide feedback:

- Paraphrase what you heard. "What I'm hearing is . . ." "Sounds like you are saying . . .";
- Ask questions to clarify points;
- Occasionally summarize the speaker's comments.

Defer judgment:

- Be patient when you don't understand;

- Allow the speaker to finish;
- Do not interrupt with arguments.

> "Applause is the only appreciated interruption"
> (Arnold Glasgow).

Respond appropriately:

- Acknowledge the speaker's feelings;
- If you find yourself responding emotionally, ask for more information. "I may not be understanding you correctly and find myself taking what you said personally. What I thought you just said was . . . . Is that what you meant?"
- Be candid, open, and honest in your response;
- Give your opinions respectfully;
- Treat the other person as you would like to be treated.

Large Assemblies

Keeping communication simple is very effective. Since lighteners only absorb part of what they hear, leaders should give information in small sections, step-by-step, and in logical order. Be creative when you communicate. Use different examples and ways to express the information. Remind folks of what you have told them without seeming repetitive. There is an axiom that goes:

1. tell them what you are going to tell them;
2. tell them what you want them to know (your message);
3. tell them what you told them.

It is okay to ask for feedback on the hearers' understanding of what you have said. That way, misunderstandings can be cleared up before they cause problems.

Notes

> Stand up straight so your audience will see you.
> Speak loudly so they will hear you. And sit down quickly
> so they will like you.

SPEECH: PATTERNS AND PRONUNCIATION

It is a good practice to review what you plan to say so that your communication will be clear. Listen to yourself speak. Listen for distracting speech patterns that include phrases such as "you know," "uh," "and that," or "and such."

Another way to prepare is to look up the pronunciation of difficult or unfamiliar words. This is especially helpful when reading scripture as there are sometimes unfamiliar words in the Bible. Look them up online or in a dictionary to find the proper way to pronounce them, and then practice.

GESTURES AND BODY LANGUAGE

Body language is non-verbal communication. It includes facial expressions, gestures, eye contact, and posture. Observing the body language of our listeners can tell us if they are interested, bored, confused, or in disagreement.

If you are speaking before a group, be sure to stand up straight. Don't lean on anything. If you are unable to stand for long periods, request permission to sit.

Avoid using gestures that may be distracting. Have someone you know observe your gestures or have yourself videotaped. Make a conscious effort to keep your hands still except to make a specific point.

EYE CONTACT

It is important in conversation and while speaking to make eye contact. Avoid staring at someone, but be sure to look at your listener(s) frequently. If you are speaking to a large group, look at the crowd but look directly at a few people in different parts of the audience. When giving a speech, be well enough prepared that you are not looking constantly at your notes. When speaking to a small group or in one-on-one conversations, be sure to engage the listeners by making eye contact.

HUMOR

Humor is good, but too much is not. Be sure that it is appropriate for the context and the culture of those to whom you are speaking. Don't assume that everyone shares your opinions about certain subjects. Once during a large conference, the main host for the conference made a "joke" about one of the performing groups. While he thought it was funny, the joke offended many people. Even though he apologized for his lack of sensitivity, his use of humor left a bad impression on many of the attendees. Do not use political humor because not everyone has the same political views, even if they are like-minded on other issues.

CULTURAL CONSIDERATIONS AND CONTEXT

Know your audience. Good communication occurs when there is a relationship or at least an understanding of the culture or attitudes of the audience. This is the context, the surrounding environment or culture of the group or individual.

In some cultures, making direct eye contact is not appropriate and may be considered offensive. Also, standing too close to people while speaking to them may be inappropriate or offensive. Be sensitive to differences that may exist in acceptable speech patterns and body language.

OTHER WAYS WE COMMUNICATE

We communicate in many ways that are less formal than the ways we have discussed so far. Communication may be as simple as a smile or giving someone a thumbs-up sign. We communicate our

Notes

Notes

faith by how we treat others and by how we live our lives. A statement attributed to Saint Francis of Assisi says, "Preach the gospel at all times. If necessary, use words."

Ministry in Daily Life

It isn't just attending church on Sundays that shows people we are Christians. How we exhibit our beliefs and walk our talk the other six days of the week is a witness as well. There is often a disconnect between what we do on Sunday and what we do Monday through Saturday. There are things we can do in our everyday lives that will witness to those around us no matter what our daily tasks.

If we carry our Bibles around with us but are rude to others, what kind of a message do we send? If we have a religious bumper sticker on our car but cut off others in traffic, what does that really say about us? We must be intentional about living our faith every day.

WAYS TO MAKE A DIFFERENCE

There are ways that, as Christians, we can make a difference in our workplaces and world. We can engage in:

> **A Ministry of Competence:** We witness to our faith by doing our jobs well. Whatever it is that we are doing—running a household, driving a cab, or working as a teacher or a healthcare worker—when we do our jobs to the best of our abilities, we are showing others that we believe we are called to work as if we were working for the Lord. Martin Luther King Jr. said, "If you are a street sweeper, be the best street sweeper you can be!"
>
> **A Ministry of Caring:** Be attentive and responsive to the needs and hurts of people around us.

We don't have to quote scripture or spout off spiritual metaphors. But we do need to care for those with whom we interact. Perhaps we listen to a co-worker who is having a difficult time or tell our boss that we will pray for the company or actually pray with someone who is receptive.

A Ministry of Ethics: Bring God's principles into the workplace. Develop a policy of integrity and honesty in all that you do.

A Ministry of Change: Help develop systems that assist all people to do their best. Work for peace, reconciliation, and justice. Exhibit grace, forgiveness, and mercy to those with whom you interact.

Whether we work in the home or are retired or work the graveyard shift in a factory, we can do all of these things to make a difference where we are.

SHARING OUR FAITH STORY

When people around us notice that we are different (and hopefully they will notice), they may ask why. What is it that makes us respond with grace to irritable customers? How can we remain so calm when everything is so hectic?

This is our opportunity to give a reason for our grace and calm or whatever fruit of the spirit we have shown. This is our chance to share the story of our faith with someone and to witness to the power of God at work in our lives. In order to have this opportunity, we must truly act differently. We must be willing to be in relationship with others and ready to tell what a difference believing in Jesus Christ makes to us.

We don't have to be preachers or biblical scholars to tell others how our faith has changed our lives and how belief in God helps us through the rough times. All we have to do is tell our story, the story of our lives lived in the light of Christ. Remember

Notes

Notes

that it is God who brings people to faith. We are the conduit, the witness, and the example. We are called to tell others. What they do with what we tell them is between them and God.

Spend time thinking about your faith journey and how you would explain it to someone if he or she asked. Think about how you could share Jesus with someone.

Biblical Reflection

> But how are they to call on one in whom they have not believed? And how are they to believe in one of whom they have never heard? And how are they to hear without someone to proclaim him? And how are they to proclaim him unless they are sent? As it is written, "How beautiful are the feet of those who bring good news!" . . . So faith comes from what is heard, and what is heard comes through the word of Christ (Romans 10:14-15, 17).

Think about people you know—friends, family, or neighbors who need to hear the Good News.

1. How will they hear it?

2. Who will tell them?

3. If you were to tell them, what would you say or do?

4. What are some ways that you can share your faith without preaching or quoting scripture?

Session Five

Into the World

Now the eleven disciples went to Galilee, to the mountain to which Jesus had directed them. When they saw him, they worshipped him; but some doubted. And Jesus came and said to them, "All power in heaven and on the earth has been given to me. Go therefore and make disciples of all nations, baptizing them in the name of the Father and of the Son and of the Holy Spirit, and teaching them to obey everything that I have commanded you. And remember, I am with you always, to the end of the age" (Matthew 28: 16-20).

Learning Outcome Goals

At the end of this session participants will be able to:

1. Describe their roles in fulfilling the Great Commission;
2. Discuss the importance of continued study and spiritual growth in the lives of Christian leaders;
3. Discover the important role of hospitality in the church;
4. Briefly describe some tools for ministry.

Notes

The Great Commission

Matthew 28:16-20 may come at the end of a gospel, but it is the beginning of Christian faith in action. Jesus originally gave this personal instruction to eleven disciples, but it has continued to be a command for all Christians throughout the ages. It is still as binding as when it was given long ago. Jesus still calls his followers to act upon their faith and spread the Good News of salvation near and far. Christians are instructed to teach others about Jesus, and we are comforted in the knowledge that Jesus will be with us to help us through the power of the Holy Spirit.

When we obey this commission to reach out to others, it changes our spiritual lives. We grow stronger in our own faith when we share it, whether it is with our neighbors or with strangers halfway around the world. Because this command is still binding, every Christian must be actively involved in some way. As lay speakers and leaders, we are called to help others realize and respond to this commission. By using our spiritual gifts in our areas of passion, we are able to spread the gospel throughout the world.

FORMS OF MINISTRY

Because we are not all gifted the same nor do we all have the same areas of passion, there are numerous ways in which we can follow this commission and make a difference in this world for Jesus Christ. Not all of us are called to preach, teach, or even lead meetings. But we are all called to serve.

There are many different courses in *Learning & Leading* that can help you discover your gifts and prepare you for service and for leading others.

The opportunities for mission and ministry are too numerous to mention here. First discover your gifts and identify your passion; then become better equipped for serving. For ideas on areas of ministry, check the *Lay Ministry Equipping Resources* catalog. (Call GBOD customer service at 1.800.972.0433 to order this catalog.)

Continuous Study and Spiritual Renewal

There is so much more room for you to grow in your faith and in your abilities as a leader. This course is the beginning; it is an introduction to a life-long learning process. We should always seek to learn and grow in our faith and find new ways to serve. If we ever think that we know it all, we are in grave danger!

Through participation in this course, you have taken the steps to improve your leading, your mission, and or your ministry. The advanced courses listed in the *Lay Ministry Equipping Resources* catalog provide a way to improve your service continuously. At least one (and sometimes two) new courses are published every year. Older courses are revised as needed to keep them current and appropriate.

There are other ways that you can continue your learning and grow spiritually. *Disciple Bible Study*, The Walk to Emmaus, The Academy for Spiritual Formation, Covenant Discipleship groups, and Stephen Ministry are all studies or experiences that will help you as you go on to perfection. There are many other ways that you can continue to grow spiritually and in knowledge. Take advantage of courses offered through your district or annual conference. Share these opportunities with others in your congregation or circle of friends. Remember that part of your responsibility is not just to grow yourself but to help others grow as well.

A Day Apart

An important part of spiritual renewal involves taking time to spend with God by reading, praying, and meditating. Set aside a period of time where there are no distractions and focus on your relationship with God. It doesn't have to cost anything but your time. Neglecting to do this will lessen your spiritual well-being. It is especially important as you step into your role as a leader to take the time to re-focus your thoughts and listen to the voice of God. "Be still and know that I am God" (Psalm 46:10).

Notes

Notes

Ongoing Outreach

Don't stop at your local church level in your mission and ministry. Look for ways to go beyond the walls and windows and into the community and the world. Search for ways that you and your congregation might make a difference to those outside your church building and membership.

If you don't find a place to use your gifts in your church, seek ways to use them in other venues. Do not let resistance in your church leadership keep you from following the Great Commission! Spend time discerning God's will and the needs that you see. In his book *Experiencing God*, Henry Blackaby says that we are to look to see where God is at work and then join God in that work.

HOSPITALITY

> Do not neglect to show hospitality to strangers, for by doing that some have entertained angels without knowing it (Hebrews 13:2).

We must be willing to welcome strangers, not only into our communities, but also into our churches. How will they know we are there if we don't invite them, if we are not a presence in the community?

Often, congregations think that they are friendly, and they are—to each other! But let a stranger come in, and they may not even speak to that person let alone welcome him or her.

Open Hearts, Open Minds, Open Doors is an advertising campaign from United Methodist Communications. It was created to invite the hurting and searching people of the world to our United Methodist churches. In our churches people will find "Open Hearts" evidenced by our theology and service in the world; "Open Minds" evidenced in our focus on servanthood; "Open Doors" that allow for a variety of understandings within one faith. Congregations may not suddenly develop these open hearts, minds, and doors, but they can "act as if" they embody these characteristics. Just as John Wesley was taught to "preach faith until you have it," our churches can begin acting as if they truly have open hearts, minds, and doors until they do have them.

Sometimes, our churches are not even listed in the phonebook. Imagine seeing a national ad for the United Methodist Church and then trying to find one locally. It can be difficult. If we really want people to come, why do we make it difficult to find us, and why don't we welcome them when they do arrive? As a lay speaker, you may make a difference in this effort in your church, district, or annual conference by speaking up and working to improve our welcome to strangers. You can promote the "Living Our Promise" training that will help churches become aware of the need to become more welcoming congregations. For more information on Open Hearts, Open Minds, Open Doors, and the Living Our Promise training, go to www.ignitingministries.org.

Hospitality goes beyond inviting and welcoming. It also includes helping strangers or newcomers find their way in the community. You may have the gifts and passion for implementing a Justice for Our Neighbors program (General Board of Global Ministries) or for finding ways that your congregation can provide resources for the poor and new citizens in the area surrounding the church.

If we are the Body of Christ why aren't we reaching out to the least and the lost? Why are we so inwardly focused on our church members and our church buildings? Look around you: where is God working? How can you or your congregation be the presence of Christ in that place? How can you truly exhibit Open Doors, Open Hearts, and Open Minds?

Appreciative Inquiry

Appreciative inquiry is a tool that we can use to help us improve our service to others. The basic principle of Appreciative inquiry is focusing on what is working well versus the usual focus on what

Notes

Notes

is wrong or not working. Our ministry planning and evaluation processes often involve:

- a description of the undesirable situation;
- a diagnosis—"what's wrong" with the system, what's not working, and why;
- a prescription to "fix what's wrong" as a "solution" that provides the way forward.

Behind most change-management or problem-solving assumptions about the way forward (getting from the current reality to the shared vision) there are often additional assumptions that focus on:

- what we do *not* have;
- our lack of resources;
- our failure to achieve;
- our "neediness."

In reality, something works in every society, organization, or group. Often, what we focus on becomes our reality. Do we focus on our problems and deficits, or on our successes and assets?

Using appreciative inquiry changes the way we look at the facts. The type of questions we ask influences the group we are asking. For instance, do we say, "What have we been doing wrong? We have not had any new members this year." Or do we say, "There were twenty visitors in our church this year. How can we make them feel more welcome?" The act of asking questions in a positive way influences the group.

Another principle is that people have more confidence to journey to the future when they carry forward parts of the past. If we look at what we have done well and focus on how we can do it better, this process results in a positive attitude of encouragement rather than discouragement. If we carry parts of the past forward, they should be what is best about the past (Sue Annis Hammond, *The Thin Book of Appreciative Inquiry* [Bend, OR: Thin Book Publishing Co., 1998], 20-21).

Traditional Problem Solving

1. "Felt Need" (Identifying the Problem)
2. Analysis of Causes
3. Analysis of Possible Solutions
4. Action Planning (Treatment)

Basic Assumption: An organization is a problem to be solved.

Appreciative Inquiry

1. Appreciating and Valuing the Best of "What Is"
2. Envisioning "What Might Be"
3. Dialoguing "What Should Be"
4. Innovating "What Will Be"

Basic Assumption: An organization is a mystery to be embraced.

Affirmative Topic Choice

There is a process that takes the affirmative topic you are discussing from *identifying* it to *creating* what it will be. This process is called the 4D cycle. We can use the 4D cycle to take the affirmative topic "We have visitors and want to be more welcoming" from an appreciation to a created reality. We start with Discover—appreciating what is (the current reality, "we have visitors"); then we move to Dream—imagine what might be (a vision, "do the visitors come back and become members?"). Then we want to move that vision toward reality by Design (what should happen, "how we will get there" and goals, "ways we can be more welcoming", "Do we need training?"); then we move to Deliver (actually make it a reality, "The congregation is more welcoming and visitors are starting to come back and becoming members"). As you deliver the new reality, the process

Notes

Notes

continues with ongoing assessments as you again appreciate what is happening, what it could be, etc. (Sue Annis Hammond, *The Thin Book of Appreciative Inquiry* [Bend, OR: Thin Book Publishing Co., 1998]).

Asset-Based Community Development

Asset-Based Community Development (ABCD) is another tool that is based on the positive aspects of current reality. Rather than focusing on the deficiencies of a community, it focuses on the assets or positive attributes and resources that are available. Instead of looking at the negative aspects, it looks at the positive. ABCD helps us find ways to work with other partners when planning our mission and ministry.

Imagine connecting with the community when we find that we need other resources. Most programs try to identify needs, design services, make or serve consumers, and give answers. ABCD focuses on people. ABCD asks questions, identifies gifts and motives, mobilizes resources into action, and develops citizens rather than consumers (from Green and Moore, *ABCD Training Group*).

ABCD principles:

- Ask and learn about gifts;
- Discover motivation to act;
- Mobilize those most able and willing to act on what you share in common;
- Keep asking questions, keep discovering possible leaders, and keep building relationships!

ABCD assumes that:

- Everyone has gifts;
- One-on-one relationships are the key;
- Real leaders have followers;

- Institutions lead best by serving citizens;
- Everyone really DOES care;
- People, associations, and institutions act on what they care about.

Both Appreciative Inquiry and Asset-Based Community Development start from an assessment of:

- What has worked well in the past (peak experiences);
- What's working now;
- What might be possible;
- The gifts (assets and relationships) we now have or can connect with to help us live into a much more optimal working environment.

Can you see this working in your church or community? Can you imagine what mission and ministry would be like if we would use all of the assets that God has provided for us instead of worrying about those we think we don't have? As a leader within your church and community, remember to focus on what has gone well, what resources are available, and how you can use these to serve the world in new and effective ways.

Conclusion

This course probably has given you a lot to think about. Hopefully it has also given you tools and information to equip you for vital ministry. Thanks be to God for your faith and your willingness to serve in the name of Jesus Christ.

> "Now to him who by the power at work within us is able to accomplish abundantly far more than all we can ask or imagine, to him be glory in the church and in Christ Jesus to all generations, forever and ever. Amen" (Ephesians 3:20-21).

Now, GO and make disciples!

Notes

Notes

Biblical Reflection

Now the eleven disciples went to Galilee, to the mountain to which Jesus had directed them. When they saw him, they worshipped him; but some doubted. And Jesus came and said to them, "All power in heaven and on the earth has been given to me. Go therefore and make disciples of all nations, baptizing them in the name of the Father and of the Son and of the Holy Spirit, and teaching them to obey everything that I have commanded you. And remember, I am with you always, to the end of the age" (Matthew 28: 16-20).

Jesus gave these instructions to his disciples. It was not an option but a commandment.

1. How do you see your role in making disciples?

2. In what ways can you use your gifts to fulfill this Great Commission?

3. What preparation do you need to follow this commandment?

A Brief History of Lay Speaking

Lay Speakers, or their predecessor Exhorters, have been around since the very earliest days of the Methodist movement. The records of the Methodist Conference of 1746 in Great Britain specifically mention Exhorters as requiring clergy approval for the office. John Wesley did not trust laity in the role of preachers or in the handling of any pastoral prerogative unless they proved themselves worthy first. When Methodism moved to America and followed the nation in its westward expansion, there were few clergy, and those were circuit riders who rode throughout large areas preaching, teaching, and baptizing. In order to survive, Methodism had to become a lay-led movement.

At the Christmas Conference of 1784 when the Methodist Episcopal Church was formally organized, the office of Exhorter was already there. The Exhorter could do sermons, lead prayer meetings, exhort, and certain other things, but not administer sacraments. Preachers had to license them. They were not preachers.

When Methodism split into two denominations prior to the Civil War, both the Methodist Episcopal and Methodist Episcopal Church South had Exhorters. While it is not clear if women were allowed to hold office, the Methodist Episcopal South *Discipline* of 1934 clearly forbids women to be Exhorters. In 1939, the two Methodist Episcopal denominations and the

Notes

Methodist Protestant Church merged to form The Methodist Church. The *Discipline* of 1944 was the last to mention Exhorters alone.

The *Disciplines* of 1948 and 1952 mentioned both Exhorters and Lay Speakers. Exhorters were licensed; Lay Speakers were certified. Per the *Discipline* of 1948, Lay Speakers could lead worship, exhort, lead prayer meetings, and needed to be reviewed or examined annually. The *Discipline* of 1952 contained the last mention of the office of Exhorter.

The *Discipline* of 1956 referred to Lay Speakers only. The *Discipline* of 1964 added conference and district committees on Lay Speaking. In 1968, the Methodist Church and the Evangelical United Brethren Church merged to form the United Methodist Church. The *Discipline* of 1968 was the first to admit women formally as either pastors or Lay Speakers. The Evangelical United Brethren Church came into the merger with a Lay Speaking history as well. According to the 1972 *Discipline*, the Lay Speaking course was eighteen to twenty hours.

The *Discipline* of 1984 was the first to show two separate levels in Lay Speaking, Basic and Certified. By the *Discipline* of 1992, the requirements of the two had pretty much been set as they are now.

It would be wrong to say that the evolution of Lay Speaking Ministries went smoothly and uniformly over the years throughout Methodism. Lay Speaking Ministries has come to us through many fits and starts, and its application and progress have varied from district to district and conference to conference. In 1993, a conclave of district and conference directors of Lay Speaking Ministries was held in Atlanta. It was repeated on a larger scale in 1995 and from thereon in odd-numbered years at Scarritt-Bennett Center in Nashville. Out of those conclaves, a budding organization of conference directors in the Southeast Jurisdiction and a group of dedicated conference directors from all jurisdictions recognized the need for more and better communication.

In January 2000, in St. Louis, the Annual Conference Directors of Lay Speaking Ministries was officially organized. The organization has strived to bring about consistency in district and conference programs and to improve communication. As of the *Discipline* of 2000, conference directors are, according to the constitution of the United Methodist Church, now members of their annual conferences just as the conference lay leaders are members. The hub of this organization operates from the office of the Director of Lay Leadership Development at the General Board of Discipleship.

(For more information, see James W. Lane, Roger D. Carlson—*A Brief History of the Office of Lay Speaker in the United Methodist Church* (1998). You may also contact the Director of Lay Leadership Development at the General Board of Discipleship, Nashville, Tennessee.)

Notes

Notes